CRITICAL THINKING

Effective Strategies That Will Make You Improve Critical Thinking And Decision Making Skills

By Gerard Johnson

TABLE OF CONTENTS

Introduction

Chapter 1 - The Building Blocks of Critical Thinking

When Do You Use Critical Thinking?

Critical Thinking Skills

Why do we need Critical Thinking Skills?

Effective Communication

Asking the Right Questions

Opens Up the Mind

Chapter 2 - Asking Questions and Critical Thinking

Types of Questions

Knowledge Questions

Comprehension Questions

Application Questions

Analysis Questions

Evaluation Questions

Synthesis Questions

The Logic Behind Critical Thinking

Chapter 3 - Implementing Critical Thinking in Your Life

Stage One: Unreflective

Stage Two: Challenged

Stage Three: Beginning

Stage Four: Practicing

Stage Five: Advanced

Stage Six: Master

Powerful Strategies to Improve Critical Thinking

Take Out Time

Deal with One Problem at a Time

Keep A Journal

Change Your Perspective

Chapter 4 - Emotional Intelligence and Critical Thinking

Self-Management

Self-Awareness

Empathy

Motivation

Social Skills

Conflict Resolution

A Living Example – Using Emotional Intelligence for Critical Thinking

Chapter 5 - 7 Key Strategies to Improve Problem Solving and Logical Thinking

Delve Deeper into the Question

Make Use of Diagrams

Attempt Logical Games

Consider your Assumptions

Choose the Right People Around You

Read Logical Books

Investigate Everything

Chapter 6 - The Importance of Independent Thinking

A Living Example – Handling The Summer Heat

Conclusion

Legal & Disclaimer

Legal & Disclaimer

The information contained in this book is not designed to replace or take the place of any form of medicine or professional medical advice. The information in this book has been provided for educational and entertainment purposes only.

The information contained in this book has been compiled from sources deemed reliable, and it is accurate to the best of the Author's knowledge; however, the Author cannot guarantee its accuracy and validity and cannot be held liable for any errors or omissions. Changes are periodically made to this book. You must consult your doctor or get professional medical advice before using any of the suggested remedies, techniques, or information in this book.

Upon using the information contained in this book, you agree to hold harmless the Author from and against any damages, costs, and expenses, including any legal fees potentially resulting from the application of any of the information provided by this guide. This disclaimer applies to any damages or injury caused by the use and application, whether directly or indirectly, of any advice or information presented, whether for breach of contract, tort, negligence, personal injury, criminal intent, or under any other cause of action.

Introduction

I want to thank you and congratulate you for buying the book, ***Critical Thinking***.

This book contains proven steps and strategies on how to become a successful critical thinker, to master problem solving and logical thinking.

The term critical thinking is used in a variety of topics for the purpose of explaining decision making, logical thinking and problem solving. For many, it is an elusive concept, yet, it can successfully be applied to solving a myriad of issues once it has been adequately applied to a situation. Critical thinking can be used in every aspect of life, including in business, personally and socially. With critical thinking, your ability to make well informed and reasonable decisions is a reality.

Critical thinking is layered in nature, with more than one-dimension present. This is because as you break down an issue or problem that you are dealing with, you begin to see it in various elements which are interrelated and come together as a whole. Think of the human body and the way that it functions. There is no simple answer to explain how you eat, breath, think and feel. If you try to understand the various elements that make you an operational human being, you will realize that you are functioning due to your digestive system, respiratory system, nervous system and so on. Then, you can go deeper into the contribution of each system to your overall well-being. This is what critical thinking embodies, looking at problem solving in a deeper way, that is logical and based on reasoning.

Critical thinking brings about excellent resolutions to problems, yet, it needs to be developed so that it can work, which requires you to have a sound strategy for success. Read on to find out how you can make critical thinking a part of your life, and how to improve your approach to problem solving and logical thinking.

Thanks again for downloading this book, I hope you enjoy it!

Chapter 1

The Building Blocks of Critical Thinking

For decades, decision making has been bilateral in nature, in that it was either 'black' or 'white'. This means that decision makers would staunchly believe that something was right or wrong. Modern times have introduced a new angle to decision making, one that takes into consideration the fact that there could be several shades of grey. Arriving at these shades of grey is not simple, as a certain amount of logic, relevance and analysis is considered. At the core of the process is critical thinking.

There are many ways one can define critical thinking. Some say that it is the process that begins with the conceptualization and application of information. This goes on to analysis and evaluation of said information, and from this, a belief is formed or an action taken. To get the information, one needs to observe what is happening around them, relate this to a specific experience, reflect on the outcome and communicate their final decision. Critical thinking can be applied to a host of subject matter.

Another definition states that critical thinking requires certain skills including honesty, rationality, open-mindedness, discipline, self-awareness and judgement. With all these in mind, it becomes possible to analyze data in order to arrive at a conclusion.

One more definition refers to critical thinking as a way of expanding the way one thinks, in a bid to improve the quality of their thoughts. This calls for considering a subject or an issue, and then analyzing and assessing it, using self-motivation and self-discipline. The result of critical thinking is the ability to see things from various points of view and have a clear and precise solution to problems, as well as being able to communicate these solutions effectively to other people.

These are just some of the definitions that exist for critical thinking, though they do have some things in common. To begin with, one must see things differently, looking at them in more detail before making a decision. This requires the information that is available to be deeply analyzed and researched, and once all the information has been considered, it becomes possible to take action. Critical thinking thus, is the best way that one can arrive at an informed decision.

When Do You Use Critical Thinking?

These broad definitions may leave you wondering when you should actually use critical thinking. Would it be better when faced with complex decisions, or on a day to day basis? The truth is, you can use critical thinking at any time or situation, as it is so flexible in its applications. When making your decision, you will consider your critical thinking skills which will lead to certain responses.

Critical Thinking Skills

Critical thinking does not occur automatically, as it needs motivation to move it forward. It also requires the culmination of special skills which together are able to bring about magnificent and well thought out results. The primary skill that you need is analytical. This skill enables you to look at a situation or scenario, and then break it into several parts, so that you can understand the nature of the situation, its function, and any relationships that it may affect.

Following analysis, you need the skill of applying standards. As you do so, you should be able to make judgements, based on certain criteria. These criteria could be personal, social or professional in nature. From the criteria that you select, you need to be able to discriminate, so that you can tell whether there are any similarities or differences in the situations that you are trying to understand.

The next skill that is needed deals with seeking information from a reliable source. This information should be holistic in nature, covering both historical and current data, as well as being both objective and subjective. The information will be scrutinized using logical reasoning, where an inference or conclusion can be appropriately supported.

These skills will bring you towards two final skills, which are predicting where you envision the plan that you are working towards and all the consequences that could result, and transforming knowledge, which change the form of your condition so that it can be relevant in a new scenario.

You can use these skills when you are creating a strategic plan, writing an article, brainstorming or using creative thinking for a task, making a scientific deduction, asking questions to arrive at a viable solution, or when making an argument on ethics. Critical thinking is the best way to ensure that your point of view is well received and backed up with the right information.

A look at these skills helps you understand the layers that are involved in making a decision or judgement based on critical thinking, and understand why it is necessary to develop these skills over time. A critical thinker needs to have the wish to go through information in detail and follow concrete evidence before arriving at any conclusion. These critical analysis skills should be mastered first, then, combined with the right attitude towards deep thought and inquisitiveness, critical thinking becomes possible.

Why do we need Critical Thinking Skills?

If you have never thought about critical thinking in detail before, you may be asking yourself why you need to have any critical thinking skills in the first place. Well, when it comes to problem solving, using critical skills is the best way to arrive at a logical and supported conclusion.

When you do not use critical thinking skills for problem solving, then you will find that it is easier to fail from making terrible decisions. Problem solving calls for making a decision while taking into consideration an element of risk. Through critical thinking, this risk can be analyzed so that all outcomes are thought of and anticipated, making it possible to deal with any consequence that result. It is like going into battle knowing that win or lose, you will have a way forward. Other benefits that come from critical thinking include: -

Effective Communication

Once an issue has been critically analyzed, it becomes possible to effectively communicate the right solution. This is especially relevant when the issue at hand is complex, requiring deep and intuitive thinking that is based on problem solving.

Asking the Right Questions

To get the best solution to any situation, you need to be able to ask the right questions, in a way that the question is both clear and precise. With critical thinking skills, you are able to logically reason through all possible variables, so that the question asked is supported by viable information.

Opens Up the Mind

Critical thinking makes it easier for you to be open-minded, as you learn to evaluate alternatives and understand the assumptions and implications of a situation. When you have an open mind, finding the solutions to problems which are complex in nature becomes considerably easier.

Critical thinking helps you to reason in a logical way, as well as to make wise decisions and solve problems. The next chapter describes how you can improve your critical thinking skills.

Chapter 2

Asking Questions and Critical Thinking

An effective critical thinker understands the benefit of being able to ask questions to arrive at a conclusion. When considering the questions to be asked, it is essential to understand that there are no questions too simple or irrelevant as part of the process. For many, there is resistance when it comes to asking questions, as having a questioning mind is often associated with lacking in intelligence or being ignorant. For the critical thinker, there is an understanding, that in asking questions, you are able to create an entire story, step by step, so that you arrive at the best conclusion.

Types of Questions

The types of questions that are asked are also important. The reason being that critical thinkers are trying to get to the heart of an issue, and are therefore not willing to take information simply at face value. This is because these questions will be based on your own thinking processes, so you must be careful to be fair, objective and honest which will enable you to move outside defining perspectives or prejudices. That way, you receive a response that is not biased. The questions you ask should also call for you to move away from your own egocentricism. Critical thinking questions should include: -

Knowledge Questions

These questions are the first ones that you ask when going through the critical thinking process. They are meant to help recollect facts and concepts, as well as allow one to give their opinion of the situation. They include questions that start with what, when, how and why. By the time you have answered these questions, you will be better able to frame your problem and put it into perspective.

Comprehension Questions

These are designed to help you bring forth your understanding of certain ideologies, so that you are able to provide information in your own words. Here, you could ask questions that start with - explain in your own words, what is the evidence that, or how would you contrast...? When you do this with information, it makes it possible to see how you understand an issue. If your understanding seems flawed or is not based on fact at this juncture, you can alter it to help you come up with a better solution later.

Application Questions

Application questions are all about being able to apply your existing knowledge and what you have learned to a new scenario or situation. These questions could include - what examples do you have, what could happen if, what methods would you use...? A critical thinker should not be biased, though, there is value on drawing on knowledge that you have. It makes it easier to break down a problem in a bid to find a solution.

Analysis Questions

These questions are all about identifying what are the causes of a situation through establishing supportive evidence. They call for the division of information into different parts, so that questions such as how can you classify or categorize, and identify the various parts can be answered. From the questions on analysis, it becomes possible to identify relationships that are internal. By this juncture, your problem has been disseminated so that you can address one part at a time. This makes it probable to arrive at a well-rounded solution.

Evaluation Questions

These are the questions that make it possible for you to come up with a judgement that is based on certain standards or definitive criteria. The evaluation questions will call for comparisons, making a choice to determine which option would be better and backing up recommendations with information. Here, you are considering different points of view, and working to determine whether your point of view has all the information required for the problem at hand. You will find that getting additional information may help you solve the problem faster.

Synthesis Questions

The synthesis questions bring together all the facts into one solution or find a new way to understand a situation based on all the facts coming together. Through this, the primary solution can be identified, as can a range of other alternative solutions. The type of question that you could ask at this stage would be about alternative solutions or interpretations.

A critical thinker will approach an issue by taking the time to go through each of these questions and then arrive at a solution. This means that the way information is analyzed within the mind is conscious, and there is a strong foundation to support the thoughts.

The Logic Behind Critical Thinking

Critical thinking is a result of logical reasoning, which means that the conclusion of an argument is based on the premise of the argument. This means that a critical thinker is able to rationally evaluate information, and must have the ability to reason with the information presented before them.

For purposes of clarification, here are some examples to consider.

Statement 1

All cheetahs are animals. Some animals hibernate, therefore all cheetahs hibernate.

The following example reveals that following critical thinking without applying logic and questions could lead to a result that is wrong. The result becomes invalid as the argument fails to take into consideration other factors, particularly because the word 'some' is used.

Statement 2

Peter is a human being. All human beings have a brain. Therefore, Peter has a brain.

This is an example of critical thinking, where logic takes center stage. The conclusion that Peter has a brain is based on the premise that he is a human being. With the information available, this makes sense.

Statement 3

Peter is a light sleeper. Peter works at Microsoft Inc. All employees of Microsoft Inc. are light sleepers.

In this example, critical thinking has taken place, however, there is no proper application of logic and reasoning to the results. This means that the argument presented is not valid, as the conclusion cannot be a fully truthful reflection of the sleeping patterns of Microsoft employees.

Looking at the statements above makes it possible to review critical thinking in relation to logical reasoning and having the right information at hand. A critical thinker will not arrive at a conclusion without properly reviewing the facts, and seeking as much information on the problem as possible. You can use logic as the basis of your critical thinking, but before you arrive at the final conclusion, it is imperative that you apply rationale and reasoning. Doing so ensure that you fully embody the process of critical thinking.

Chapter 3

Implementing Critical Thinking in Your Life

To experience the full effects of critical thinking, you need to come up with strategies that will enable you to implement critical thinking in your life. You should not view critical thinking as an activity that you do once off, when facing an issue. Your end goal should be to make critical thinking a part of your life. Once you do so, you can expect to make clearer decisions for all problems, as well as to confidently support any decisions that you have had to make.

Furthermore, critical thinking can help you move up to your full potential, as you learn what is necessary to help you improve your thinking. It is necessary for you to be conscious to the critical thinking process, so that you train your mind to make logically and reasonably calculated thoughts, rather than simple thoughts that are based on simple facts.

As critical thinking occurs in layers, it is necessary to advance as a critical thinker by going through several stages as follows: -

Stage One: Unreflective

During this stage, you do not know that there are any problems with your current way of thinking. You have not consciously attempted any critical thinking and are living your life as you normally would. This could be described as being normal.

Stage Two: Challenged

This is the stage where you begin to question your thoughts and the way that you make decisions. It could be that you have an 'aha' moment, where you realize that your thinking may have some problems and you have the power to correct these problems. At this point, changing your point of view and actions seems like a plausible solution.

Stage Three: Beginning

At this stage, you have some self-driven actions that attempt to improve the way that you think. You will carry these out sporadically, aiming to change your thinking in certain situations, rather than change your thinking as a whole.

Stage Four: Practicing

You will have discovered that you cannot make half a commitment when it comes to improving your thinking and decision making. Therefore, instead of sporadic behavior, you become invested in consistently trying out different actions to improve your thinking and decision making.

Stage Five: Advanced

The more that you practice, the better your critical thinking skill becomes. This stage is varied in its intensity from one person to the next, as it depends on the amount of effort one is willing to put into their critical thinking practice.

Stage Six: Master

This is the nirvana of critical thinking, the stage that all critical thinkers are striving to attain. At this stage, you have mastered the skills required for critical thinking, and you are deeply insightful when it comes to making any decisions. Critical thinking has become a part of you, and is no longer a consistent effort that you make to arrive at decisions.

Powerful Strategies to Improve Critical Thinking

These critical thinking stages clearly explain the change in mind-set that you must undergo if you want to become a critical thinker. To move from one step to another, there are certain strategic behaviors you must carry out. These include: -

Take Out Time – You must invest quality time into perfecting your critical thinking time. This does not mean that you set aside hours each day to think. It does mean that when you have a moment, for example, when stuck in traffic or walking from one place to another, take that time to be more productive with your thinking. As you do this, you will begin to observe certain factors about your thought process and how you arrive at conclusions.

Deal with One Problem at a Time – Critical thinking requires your mind to be clear, so do not clutter it with trying to solve too many problems at the same time. Instead, go through one problem at a time. Doing this will enable you to clearly state the problem in your mind and understand what type of problem it is. Then, you are able to come up with several ways to solve the problem through seeking information. This makes it easy for you to interpret what you have available and arrive at a plausible solution.

Keep A Journal – Keep track of different problems that you have managed to resolve as a result of critical thinking. You need to have a format that you can follow to address each problem. Four steps that you can use are to state the problem that was faced and its significance. This should be followed by how you responded to your problem from beginning to end, taking note the critical thinking steps that you followed through the entire process. The third step is to review the way you arrived at your decision to determine whether there was anything that you left out or which could have been done better. Follow this with an assessment, where you consider the implications of the decision you arrive at. Determine whether there have been any lessons learned, and if you would approach the entire problem in a different way if you had the opportunity to do so.

Change Your Perspective – It is highly likely that you have a way of being and seeing, which is based on your personal and social interactions. From your experiences, you define the way that you understand things. For normal thinking, this is fine, yet for a critical thinker, this can be very limiting. You will find that seeing the world from one perspective means that your solutions to problems tend to also follow one pattern. Often, this can lead to frustration and negative emotions. A critical thinking needs to be able to redefine how they view the world, so that they have a more open mind. This will make it possible to find solutions in unlikely places or scenarios.

Now that you understand the stages of critical thinking, it is easier to determine the place that critical thinking has in your life. To ensure that you make use of critical thinking in the best way, lean on the strategies that make it easier. Before long, you will find that critical thinking comes to you easily.

Chapter 4

Emotional Intelligence and Critical Thinking

Emotional intelligence is linked to critical thinking, and must be mastered if one is to become an excellent critical thinker. Emotional intelligence is important for decision making as it is able to predict the success of a business, the happiness of employees and the quality of all the relationships in an organization.

When making decisions as a critical thinker, you need to look at logic, and from this logic, apply your rational and reasoning so that you arrive at the right answer. With emotional intelligence, this becomes easier. Emotional intelligence affects the following: -

Self-Management

Your decision making can be clouded by emotions that are not kept in check. With emotional intelligence, it becomes possible to manage your emotions better. This will give you more control over the decision making process. In addition, when you have to adapt your emotions and reactions, you can do so to ensure that the response you give to a problem situation helps to resolve it, rather than accentuate it.

Self-Awareness

Emotional intelligence makes you more aware of your emotions, and also helps you to understand your reactions. When you understand your reactions, you are better able to identify triggers that can cause you to react in ways that are irrational. As a critical thinker, this is necessary as arriving at a well thought out decisions requires a stable mind.

Empathy

Being able to connect with others on their level, by discerning their feelings, as well as paying heed to their emotions is another result of emotional intelligence. The critical thinker can use this type of feedback to help relate to them in a more effective way, and also create solutions that are mutually beneficial.

Motivation

A significant aspect of critical thinking and its possible success is inner motivation and commitment to the entire process. Motivation is also important in emotional intelligence as it helps you to bring together those emotions that motivate you to take a specific action, and to see a scenario through to the end so that you can achieve a specific goal

Social Skills

Great teams are able to come together due to emotional intelligence. This is because people are better able to relate to one another, as well as develop their relationships and work in a team. When you have to utilize your critical thinking skills in a group, having people who are all on the same page is an excellent advantage.

Conflict Resolution

Critical thinking can be used for solving a myriad of problems, as well as in working out an argument. When you argue using critical thinking, you are aware that there is a point of view that exists outside your own, that you have a purpose for the argument and an audience, and that it is essential to have a central issue that you are dealing with so that you can tackle it with information from key concepts. Factually and logically, this makes excellent sense, though when you input some emotion, you may end up with irrational solutions. When emotions are not well controlled, they can cloud judgement.

However, with emotional intelligence, it becomes possible to control these emotions, mainly due to empathy and being able to see things from various perspectives. This insight means that one can avoid conflicts that arise in arguments, and better negotiate for the desired results.

A Living Example – Using Emotional Intelligence for Critical Thinking

Consider the following scenario. You have just walked into a fancy clothes store and decided to try a few of the items on, so that you can have an idea on what they look like on you. You randomly pick items off the shelf, and the criteria you are making to arrive at your decision is how close it is to your arm, and the colors or design. As you try on these items, you arrive at one that makes you look stunning. It is the right shape and color and a perfect fit. You decide there and then that you will not leave the store without it. You take it off and check the price and suddenly you feel terrible. It costs four times what you are able to afford. You leave the store feeling bad.

A few days later, you have the chance to go into another clothes store to purchase some new clothing. This time, you have a different approach. The reason is you do not want to leave the store *feeling* as bad as you did the last time. You are using your emotions to guide you. You therefore adopt some critical thinking steps. You begin by carefully going through what is available and gathering information on style, design and price. With this information at hand, you are able to make a better decision, only trying on the clothes that you know you can afford. By the time you are leaving the shop, you have made a decision you are happy with.

If you did not have your emotions to guide you, then you would have lacked the logic and reasoning necessary to prevent yourself from making the same mistake you had made previously. With emotional intelligence at your fingertips, you are better able to solve your problem with self-regulation and proper decision making.

Chapter 5

7 Key Strategies to Improve Problem Solving and Logical Thinking

Critical thinking is all about solving problems, using logical thinking as a guide. When your logical thinking happens to be flawed, then you will find that solving problems can be a challenge, and that the decisions you make will not be good. Now that you know how to develop your critical thinking skills, you need some guidance on improving these skills so that they can be perfected over time. The end result is that instead of spending too much time thinking hard about a problem, you will be able to think better. Here are 7 key strategies that will guarantee you positive results with problem solving as well as logical thinking.

Delve Deeper into the Question

Starting off with a broad question will make it difficult for you to come up with the right answer, particularly when you are thinking critically. Critical thinking calls for you to examine a host of variables, following which you are then able to get to a solution. Here is an example of how you can delve deeper.

Question 1 – How can I teach a class?

This question is challenging to respond to as there are many variables that have not been explained. These include the size of the class, the type of class, the educational level and so on. Attempting to logically address this will lead you to confusion.

Question 2 – How can I teach a high school English class with 10 students?

This question is much better than the first question. It brings in certain specifics including the education level, the subject of the class and the number of students. From this, you can begin to logically come up with a solution. However, you can do even better when delving deeper into the question.

Question 3 – What are the number of high school students taking English this semester? How can I teach a high school English class with 10 students?

This helps put your response in better perspective such that you can now break your logical response into several problems. From these problems, you are better able to determine what they are attributed to such that they begin to make better sense as you continue with your critical analysis of the issue at hand.

Make Use of Diagrams

A picture speaks a thousand words and an excellent diagram can help to accentuate your logical thinking. A great mind that embodied an excellent

critical thinker was Steve Jobs from Apple. When sharing information in a presentation, he drew the audience in and helped them arrive at a conclusion by making use of illustrations and diagrams in his presentations. The type of diagrams that you should lean towards include flow charts that lay out processes, boxes which can contain information as well as represent your logic. When you have a problem to solve, try drawing it out first using a paper and pan, and then, you can apply the necessary words to find a solution. Over time, you will be able to mentally create your own flowcharts and diagrams, and influence your decision making without the need for other materials.

Attempt Logical Games

There are games that are purely based on logic if you want to arrive at a solution, such as chess and Sudoku. Chess is a great game to play with another person, as you learn to understand how other people think, and how their thoughts affect their judgements. You also develop the skills of strategy and problem solving, as you work your way across the board in an attempt to win the game.

Sudoku is a great game to play on your own, as it helps you come up with different ways that you can reason. Through this game, you learn about solving a problem by getting rid of certain variables, and using the information that you have available to help you arrive at a viable solution.

Consider your Assumptions

You will be amazed at the number of assumptions that you make before you finally arrive at a decision. Assumptions are not based on truth or something that must happen, they are instead our opinions of something that could happen if we take a certain action. When looking to improve your problem solving and logical thinking abilities, you need to be discern when your thoughts and actions are based on assumptions instead of facts. This means that you need to be able to dissect the issue.

Consider the following assumption – You go to sleep at night because you are tired. Here the assumption is that in order for you to go to sleep, you must be tired. This may not be the case. Rather than basing a result on a conclusion of this nature, it would be better to examine it more deeply, to determine the real reasons that lead to sleep, and whether this is linked to the reasons that cause one to be tired.

Choose the Right People Around You

Many people who are successful do not make it to the top because they are brilliant, they make it to the top because they are willing to invest in and hire people who are more intelligent than they are. This means that they have the best minds operating their businesses, while at the same time, they remain motivated to get the knowledge required to keep up with their staff.

When you have people smarter than you around you, it is easier to learn something from them, which will help you improve the way that you do

things, as well as build on your critical thinking skills. Their intelligence will make it necessary for you to come up with logical ways to interact and communicate with them, which will help develop the way that your brain works as well.

Read Logical Books

Read, read and read some more, and you will be amazed at how quickly you can elevate your logical reasoning. Do not read just any books. Focus on those that will get you thinking, and these books mainly fall into the category of mysteries and thrillers. As you read these books, work on figuring out what could happen by the end of the book. You may need to identify a villain, figure out what is happening with an attack, or simple solve a mystery of some sort. By looking at all the variables, you will find that making a calculated guess is not only possible, it gets easier with time. To perfect this skill, you must keep reading and keep practicing.

Investigate Everything

Every time that you receive some information, take time to do a thorough investigation to determine whether the information that you have on hand is good or not. This is applicable to all information, no matter who the source may be. When you being to investigate in this matter, your brain starts to analyze information in a different way. You will begin to see loopholes in information, and make judgements based on all that has been made available to you. This is particularly true of negative news which may be sensational rather than factual. Problem solving will become much easier, as will critical thinking when it comes to addressing issues.

These seven strategies are highly practical and easy to implement. They are also result oriented, and the more you practice them, the easier it becomes to be a critical thinker.

Chapter 6

The Importance of Independent Thinking

The best critical thinkers are independent thinkers. This is because they have a way of looking and addressing an issue that makes them stand out for being extraordinary. Having the ability to look outside the box and be different from all other thinkers is what you should be striving for as you work on your critical thinking. For this to work, you need to make certain decisions from the get go, as well as be ready to take specific steps. The decisions are as follows: -

- Be prepared to follow through with your ideas, particularly if they are not practical or appear impossible. It is highly likely you may be mocked or disregarded for having an independent thought, yet having the courage to follow through with your thought, using critical thinking strategies, will enable you to have a breakthrough.

- Be motivated to move yourself forward. As it stands, most people have similar thinking patterns and therefore, they arrive at similar conclusions. While this may be acceptable, it does not call for progress. Critical thinking helps one improve their performance, so that they can achieve more than expected, while avoiding coming up with simple and conventional solutions.

To explore independent thinking so that you can become a better critical thinker, you need to take the following steps: -

- Take some steps away from your comfort zone – Look for experiences and scenarios where you are forced to challenge and defend your point of view. This may need you to attempt interactions with those from different cultures, or to seek those who would actively oppose what you have to say. By coming up against them, you will need to logically think through solutions or ways that will enable you to win an argument. This is excellent exercise for the budding critical thinker.

- Stay away from convention – There are so many different tools that exist which are working towards controlling or steering your thoughts. These expose you to public opinion, which tends to be more conventional than independent. To develop your critical thinking skills, you need to disconnect, so that your entire analytical process is not interrupted by television, the internet or other opinions. Staying away from these conventional media will give you the room you need to see everything from your own perspective, rather than form the perspective of the masses.

- Look at what is happening around you – Many times, it is possible that you are so busy working towards finding your place in life, that you do not take the necessary time to observe what is happening around you so that you know where you fit in. Independent thinkers take the time to look at what is happening around them. Doing so can aid in critical thinking and problem solving, as it becomes possible to see things through a different perspective. Observation also means that you create room to challenge your existing beliefs, which means that you can find new ways to look at situations.

A person who has managed to master independent thinking can be described as a mature thinker, as they have mastered how to look outside the box. At this level, combined with critical thinking, one's process of problem solving can lead to heightened awareness, as well as elevated levels of joy and happiness.

A Living Example – Handling The Summer Heat

An office that has 20 workers have been asked to propose solutions on how to deal with the heat during the summer. It becomes unbearable and makes it challenging to work effectively. There are several solutions that are presented by the workers. These include allowing the staff to wear lighter clothing so that they retain less heat while at work, as well as ensuring there is plenty of cold icy water available so that workers can instantly cool themselves down with a drink. Other solutions included being able to use extra fans or strong air conditioning to keep the room cool during work hours. These ideas as all excellent and can be implemented. They are practical and for the most part, cost effective. However, one of the workers saw things differently.

This worker recommended that the management develop a new office in their adjacent property which was an empty lot. This property should be built with special materials that are designed to keep the heat out and cool air in. An office of this nature would be ideal for use in the summer for years to come. This is not the type of answer that was expected from the workers, as it is not highly practical for an immediate solution, and it will require a significant investment. Nonetheless, it is an indication that there is someone within the workers who is able to come up with an independent thought that could have lasting benefits.

This independent thought reveals evidence of critical thinking. After considering the solutions that have been posed by other staff, the independent thinking worker realized that there was need to come up with a long-term solution to the problem, rather than a stop gap measure to help staff survive the summer.

There are consequences to independent thinking as well as to the critical thinker. By changing the way you see the world and solve problems, you will bring about change in the way that things are done, or create a situation of chaos, where things seem to be going out of control. Persevering through this is important, as after all the dust settles, the final results reveal an excellent way forward.

Conclusion

Thank you again for downloading this book!

I hope this book was able to help you to improve your critical thinking skills.

The next step is to apply the strategies and techniques that you have learned in this book.

Critical thinking has often been misunderstood in various ways. The largest misunderstanding comes in believing that critical thinking is about passing judgement on other people, based on the information that you have on hand. Critical thinking is far from this, in fact, it is considerably deeper in its intent. Critical thinking is all about decision making, and helping a person get to the best possible decision following information analysis that is based on a range of perspectives.

In the chapters of this book, you have learned all about what critical thinking actually is and how you can use it in your life. In addition, you also know about the stages of critical thinking and the skills that are necessary to master critical thinking and make it a permanent part of your life. Critical thinking can be applied to every area of your life, in a professional as well as social manner. This is because you make hundreds of problem solving decisions each day, and having critical thinking at your fingertips will ensure that the decisions you make are well thought out and offer viable solutions to all problems.

With critical thinking, you stop yourself from thinking harder in order to arrive at a solution. Instead, you enjoy the benefits of thinking better, no matter what challenge that you find yourself up against.

Made in the USA
Monee, IL
28 December 2023